KATE

THE DUCHESS OF CAMBRIDGE

ROYAL FASHIONS COLORING BOOK

Eileen Rudisill Miller

DOVER PUBLICATIONS, INC.
Mineola, New York

The world watches in awe and admiration as Kate, the Duchess of Cambridge, displays her acute fashion sense in her many public appearances. Artist Eileen Rudisill Miller brings Kate's royal fashions to life in this charming coloring book. Brimming with notable designers such as Sarah Burton (for Alexander McQueen), Orla Kiely, Jenny Packham, Jane Corbett, and Alice Temperley, the detailed pages offer satisfying opportunities to recreate Kate's dresses, coats, and hats. Prince William and Prince George put in an appearance, and the newest addition to the royal family—Princess Charlotte Elizabeth Diana, born May 2, 2015—is included as well!

Bibliographical Note
Kate, the Duchess of Cambridge Royal Fashions Coloring Book is a new work, first published by Dover Publications, Inc., in 2015.

International Standard Book Number
ISBN-13: 978-0-486-79772-4
ISBN-10: 0-486-79772-4

Manufactured in the United States by RR Donnelley
79772403   2016
www.doverpublications.com

Kate chose this coat dress by Emilia Wickstead, worn with a Lock & Co. hat,
for the Irish Guards St. Patrick's Day parade.

This dusty pink Jenny Packham gown, worn to a charity gala,
is studded with Swarovski crystals.

Kate wears a dramatic red sarai silk jersey gown by Beulah London.

The Duchess of Cambridge is picture perfect in a deep purple jersey dress by Issa.

This "De Gournay Chinoiserie" hand-painted dress by Jenny Packham
features gold-toned leaves on a gray background.

Kate appears in a bright green Diane von Furstenberg "Maja" shift dress
in a visit to Los Angeles.

The Duchess wows in a lilac Sarah Burton for Alexander McQueen gown
at a celebrity-packed event.

This cream piqué frock by Alexander McQueen sports a ruffled skirt.

Kate sparkles in a blue jacquard coat dress by Jane Troughton,
topped by a Jane Corbett disc hat.

Resplendent in a red Alexander McQueen dress and James Lock & Co. hat
for the Queen's Jubilee, Kate strikes a charming pose.

A gray-and-silver floral-stitched Erdem dress is matched
with a Jane Corbett hat in the same shades.

17

Kate exudes style in a taupe wool Burberry trench coat.

This belted brown "Celeste" coat by Hobbs, worn over a black
turtleneck-style dress, is one of Kate's favorites.

Kate and Will walk the red carpet at Royal Albert Hall, Kate elegant in a teal beaded "Aspen" lace gown by Jenny Packham.

The Duchess chooses a midnight-blue chiffon gown by Jenny Packham
for the Portrait Gala.

Kate wears a blue-and-white lace metallic-embroidered Alice Temperley dress
to a Diamond Jubilee tea party.

Kate wore this brilliant green Evelyn + Lara coat by Catherine Walker
on a trip to Australia in 2014.

This white Diane von Furstenberg square-necked dress
is scattered with blue flowers.

The new mother wears Alexander McQueen's "Ivory Wave Ruffle" jacket and Jane Taylor's "Georgie" beret for the christening of Baby George on October 23, 2013. The christening gown is a replica of the one commissioned by Queen Victoria in 1841.

Kate's yellow Emilia Wickstead coat is topped by an Amanda Whitely hat.

Kate chose a bright yellow wool crepe Roksanda Ilincic dress
for a trip to Australia with William and George.

This cotton Diane von Furstenberg "Patrice" wrap dress
features a bold navy-on-white pattern.

Here are two fashion statements by Kate: a demure pink pleated Emilia Wickstead creation on the left, and a sporty lemon silk crepe frock by Jenny Packham on the right.

Kate and William present Princess Charlotte Elizabeth Diana, born on May 2, 2015, to an adoring public. Jenny Packham, the designer of Kate's dress, posted a message to the royal couple: "Congratulations to the Duke and Duchess of Cambridge . . . . The Duchess wears a bespoke silk shift dress with buttercup print."